P A  O L E

Darius Woods

Dedication

This book is dedicated to the memory of my mother, Laquita Woods, my OG Ernest Purifoy, my grandmother Peggy Purifoy and Shirley Hampton, my Step-Grandfather Harold Amos and my brother Johnnie Chapman III. They have departed in physical form, but their support, love, and guidance continue to inspire me every day.

Table of Contents

Acknowledgements

Kiara, my best friend, my lover, my ride or die continue to push me to be the best man I can be. I thank GOD for you and Denver every day!

Diviniti, you taught me how to be an overprotective brother at times lol. You helped me find ways to survive growing up, to be compassionate, and how to always be a leader. I love you.

Doris and Johnnie Chapman, All glory to the most high for you two; I wouldn't be who I am without the help and guidance from you both. I lost both parents, and y'all took me in with a genuine heart. I love you both!

Peggy P, the most fussing grandma but always wants what's best. Always speak your mind and tell it how it is, and that's where I get it from. Most loving, open-hearted woman I've ever met. From staying on me about church and staying on me about my tithes.

Because of our prayers, GOD keeps his hand over me. I will forever miss you! Love you

Jason Bobo, you taught me how to walk in my own shoes and be my own man. So much alike but in our own ways. Through any loss to keep my head up, I appreciate you G! Love. Not only were you a great real model for me, but the whole hood wanted to be like ya and I've always been proud to say that's Unk!

Keno, my brother from another, my dawg 4 life! From Crystal Palace days, from flipping on pissy mattresses, to going to school together, to growing up in the hood together, it made us even closer. From playing ball, mane the fights, to supporting each other in whatever we do. Always standing for what you believe in. I appreciate you homie a lot!! My Negu!!!

Marvell, blood couldn't make us any closer, through all our ups and downs together through childhood until present times. Through the good and the bad, forever my dawg G. Love my Negu!

Roc, my guy till infinity, you never changed up. You help make my college years the best G. To our little minor disagreements on campus and the 1 week of beef, lol I love you G fr! My Negu!

Mad Max, you know it's all love G, (chocolate) from the good to the bad to getting put in the doghouse lol we live and learn. Love my Negu!

And to my Stepdad who was taken away from his family due to violence, I appreciate you a lot. You were there in our time and needs and support from when my mama was here and when she departed even until you departed. Though all the trials and tribulations we have faced, I love ya G! Forever Missed.

Introduction

Patience is planting a seed and watching it flourish.

Patience is being good at something and developing a skill over time.

Patience is building a brand from the ground up .

Patience is waiting on a check to clear your bank account.

Patience is having a newborn being brought into this world and watching them grow.

Patience is hearing a baby cry and you have to figure out what's wrong.

Patience is rocking & trying to get your little one asleep.

Patience is living in an apartment complex and the people above you are inconsiderate.

Patience is waiting to get approved for a house.

Patience is waiting for an autopsy.

Patience is being Black in America.

Patience is being racially profiled & remaining calm.

Patience is waiting for everything that's done in the dark to come to light.

Patience is having faith of a mustard seed.

Patience is seeing a relative get killed and you have to wait till the police catch the killer.

Patience is living in a uniquely unjust world.

Patience is living in a generation of eager peers and maintaining your peace.

I choose to be at peace. I choose to let go of any emotion that doesn't serve me. Nothing and nobody can decide how I feel. I'm at ease.

Time waits on no one and you can't be afraid to jump; success starts in your mind and you have to believe in yourself first and at some point, you have to take affirmative action. God gives us all a purpose and it's up to you to discover yours, we are programmed to smile through our pain, but you ask yourself how much longer do we have to pretend. We live in poverty with drugs, guns, and gangs and no father in the household, so there's no guidance which makes some turn to the streets. The gutter makes some wiser, yet it corrupts the weak; young teens rather catch a body than learn more about their history. This book is about a young man who wanted success so badly, which made him determined; he loved his family and used sports as a gift and didn't let it use him. He found his sanctuary through his craft and continued to master it while keeping patience. It's easy to get distracted and fall off into the deep end, and if you can't swim, you will drown. There have been 323 homicides in the year 2020, breaking the 2016 homicide record. The unemployment rate is at 58% and many are living paycheck to paycheck, trying to survive and maintain their family.

In America, more than 60% of people in prison are ethnic minorities... three-fourths of all persons in prison for drug offenses are people of color...we are steadily fighting for racial justice, cops killing us and still walking free, and Fake OG's misleading the youth. I feel like if you have an "OG" that's misleading you, he's not an "OG" he's just a N***a older than you. Providing for your family is more gangster than anything, and I was told "Faith Without Work is Dead" . How can you want a Dream to happen if you don't have a work ethic? Every man thinks he's the slickest thang moving until he gets washed in the game... We all want to be successful, we all want to make money, but you shouldn't want to jeopardize your freedom for it, so just stay down and wait your turn.

Young King, born in Memphis, Tennessee, had to fight at an early age. Smart kid going places because he knows how to survive through idle time. Fell in love with sports at the age of three, from football to baseball, but ball and boxing has always been his escape. When coming from such a negative environment, many don't make it out due to negative comments and negative people, but he had it in his mind that he was going to achieve it, and nothing was going to stop him. If you put GOD first, everything else will fall in place, it's already paved for you; just follow the signs.

This kid knew he was great before everybody else saw the greatness in him because he believed in himself, confident yet humble. Being great takes time, and when growing up in a rough community, you have to use your third eye tremendously and not be easily influenced. One has to know what they want out of life, bulldoze all adversity, every obstacle and beat the statistics. Visualize success in your future and let the past be the past. The reason your windshield on your vehicle is bigger than the rearview mirror, because you can't go back and change your past, but you can predict your future which is bright. The life in front of you is far more important than the life behind ya. Once you get a better perspective on the world, your whole mindset shifts. Life is like boxing; the same way you throw a punch, you have to be able to take one as well, if you are afraid to take a punch then you are already defeated. Life will knock you down and keep you down if you let it, but you must get up and fight again; there will be hard times and you will hit some roadblocks, but just keep pushing and conquer success!

Being Great

All the Greats knew they were great before they even became great. Real G's move silent under the surface, barely talk, but you know he's in the room just by his presence. The Godfather was a silent one but spoke with volume; he also made offers that one couldn't refuse. Sometimes when he walked in a room you could hear a pin drop; he was well respected and when you get respect from others, don't too many disrespect you. See, your character will determine your faith, not your talent, basically how you treat people so what you dish out is what you will get in return. One can't be negative and expect positive things; life doesn't work like that. I can admit life is not all sunshine, rainbows and flowers, and you will not go through life without having any problems, losses into lessons learned and nobody has a blueprint to it, so just keep pushing. One has to learn not to stress over things we have no control over, and life doesn't always go as planned, but if something is meant for you, it will happen; you just have to have patience and trust the process. Every day is a challenge so you can either let your current circumstance either make you stronger or let it break you. Sometimes we ask ourselves what's the name of this roller coaster, where we have our good days and our bad days, so you have to find a balance to keep your head steady. The universe has ways of talking to us. So keep all hands, feet, and other objects inside the ride, fasten your seatbelts, and welcome to Life.

The Golden Child

O n January 9th, God brought a young king into this world and he was blessed. We are all given a purpose and this King discovered his own and mastered it. Growing up, he usually got a lot of negative criticism due to him being smaller than the average kid, but he didn't let it stop him. Instead, he turned it into a positive situation and motivated himself daily. He's been in life-death situations where he has looked the barrel of a gun down before, from him getting staples in his head from being pushed into a stove, and also a car accident that he passed out in due to the airbag Collision. Heart over Everything! [Grew up in South Memphis and the Haven area has seen a lot of tricks and trades even had some try to influence him, but he always had a mind of his own.] See, In this world, it's two types of people which are the ones that truly believe in you more than you believe in yourself and then you got the people that hate themselves, so they try to take it out on you by trying to doubt you or pull you back under because they gave up, that's Jealousy, stay away from them. See it's only 24 hours in a day and 365 days in a year it's up to you on how you utilize your time. A person's words can't control your destiny. God does, along with your work ethic! This kid worked on his craft every chance he got and took advantage of the opportunities that was presented to him [he knew what he wanted out of life when he first touched the ground on earth, but sometimes God has other plans in store for you that you knew nothing about and the plane may come to a delay with you trying to figure out your Purpose.] With the tribulations he was already facing off the court he was dealing with even more bullshit from signing a bad contract deal to losing money and also dealing with bitterness from the mother of his child.

When a mother uses a child as a pawn, that's considered very malicious, especially when he wants to be in his child's life, it's only hurting the child.

Move on, baby, let that man do for his child y'all didn't work-out. As a kid, he's been through a lot and seen a lot, him and his Dad weren't on the best terms, but he still loved him. The world will make you have a grudge towards somebody that you had no intentions of doing at all, but life humbles you right before your eyes. God places people in your life for a reason and before his dad died, he showed him the journey not to take, which made him want to build his own empire and leave his own legacy. Of course, mistakes were still made and I bumped my head a few times, went to jail for weed, almost got kicked out for fighting and gambling and even stole before. I still remember the days when we didn't have any food in the house and I had to make way for my little sister and me. At the time, those noodles, hot sauce and crackers tasted like a gourmet meal. Everybody's journey is different so you have to embrace your struggle as well, there's no testimony without a story and the struggle is going to make you who you are today so don't ever forget where you come from. One must be willing to prosper in life, though, give up on old habits and socialize with people who look more like your future and not your past. Having no father in the household is unstable at times, but it also teaches you how to think through all decisions and teaches you to man up.

When you are looking at a black man, you are looking at a GOD, black fathers are great and yes, we need them away from the system that is designed for us to fail. That's why we have to break the cycle and create generational wealth. Ok, you from the hood, ok Me too! When we die, guess what? It's still going to be "The Hood" and old memories will only surface, but people will continue to live their lives. We don't know when our last day is, so plan for your kids' future. Fuck the streets; I've seen how that story ends multiple times, especially in the black community. Establish your credit; they don't teach us any of that in school, so you should learn it and put yourself and your kids in positions to win because street credit doesn't solidify in Banks.

OG E

Life gives us all kinds of trials and tribulations, that's God preparing you ahead of time with His test and you will overcome them. I lost my dad when I was seventeen and it hurt me; he reminded me so much of Percy Miller (Master P). Our relationship wasn't just completely good, but my love for him was genuine. My dad was doing time in the state mostly throughout my high school years, but he still did his best. I'll never forget that one time he showed up to my high school game and man, that probably was one of the happiest moments of my life. We won, and I finished the game with 25 points and couldn't do anything but smile because my OG was sitting in the front row watching it. It's the simple moments that matter the most, just his presence brought more joy into the room.

During his absence, I asked him one day on a visit "Yo Dad this isn't a place to be, isn't it" he looked at me and said "hell no son it's not" I replied "so promise me you'll stay out this cage when you get out, we miss you" he just looked at me, smiled and said "I gotcha son" I later went and got him some snacks from the vending machine and enjoyed the rest of my time with him with our conversation. My dad was a cool guy down to earth and showed everybody love; he was always happy regardless of what he was going through. While my dad was doing time on the inside, I was missing him more and more on the outside and it was showing around the house. A mother can only do so much and she can't teach a boy how to be a man, she can help correct his mistakes and nurture his mind, but honestly, she can only teach him how to be a gentleman. I used to be so upset leaving my games because the kids I was playing with had their pops and outside looking in on society; they looked like a happy home with both parents. [Growing up, I never saw my Mama and Pops together, and it made me want that feeling more to raise my own. They never had anything against each other and every time they got around each other; it was always "nun but Love." My folks did a great job; my mistakes came on my behalf.] I wasn't just a good kid; I got in trouble. I did a lot of skipping in school, hustling, etc. I didn't even think I was going to graduate at one point, but I made it. God gives us our biological parents; then he also blesses people in your life to help you elevate to the next Pinnacle of Life and remain level-headed and Grateful.

Ma Dukes

A Mother will always be a Son's first love, and a Mother will always have the key to her son's heart. A Mother only wants what's best for her child, and at the time, you might not see that. You may feel like she's being negative, but really she's showing you that not everybody is going to support you but reach for the stars King. In a mother's eyes, you will forever be her baby; she will always love you no matter the age or height. She just has to instill the game (knowledge) and fearlessness in you so you won't be lost or defeated by any loss. "Pick ya head up G and keep movin; shoulders up and Chest out," I lost my Mom, and it felt like I lost everything, felt like my heart had been ripped out my body completely and thrown on the ground, the worst feeling ever. [Like a sharp butcher knife had been carved in my body from the top to the bottom.] Even years later I can still feel her loss and I can still hear her voice "Pick ya Head up G and keep movin; shoulders up and chest out." [My mama prepared me ahead of time for this, by always saying "I won't always be here" I used to be like, "Mane gone on Ima jump in the casket with ya and we are going together." She kept me mentally strong always, so from me to you regardless of the situation that you may be in now, be grateful G that you're able to wake up and just be able to breathe and smile because you're not dead, in jail, or a hospital.

My mama was a bonafide hustler professional but had a switch where she could cut up but still be under control if you tried her. She was book and street smart, carried herself as a Queen, was a firm believer of God, and preached how important education was not only for herself but also for her kids. I remember she used to have my sister and I read different books before we went to bed and give her a slight summary of what we both engaged our eyes in after. My mother and I relationship were somewhat like brother and sister, but she also lived by the scripture:

Proverbs 13:24 (a love affair is likened to a **child**, and spanking is mockingly commended as a way to make the love grow stronger...) teaches a child that you will not get accustomed of having your way and be a spoiled brat but in a summary of Quita language: play with me if you want to Ima go upside Yo head with this pan. If I can recall, I think my mom gave me 3 of the all-time great whoopings I'll never forget in history.

First for cutting up in school, Second for running from the police, Third for imitating my step-grandpa Harold with his lighter and setting his trash can on fire. My mama later came and picked me up and whooped me in the car while she was driving from white haven all the way to the exchange building downtown and then got another whooping in the house. I still have flashbacks from that one. My mom was cool as a fan but meant business when it came to disciplining her children; she felt like if she didn't do it then society would because this world owes you Nothing. The most disappointing moment I ever had with my mom was when I went to jail for weed. It hurt me more having to make that phone call to her and I knew then that wasn't for me. I later got everything expunged, but she was very upset and even gave me the cold shoulder. I also had to gain her trust back, but I love her to this day for it because it made me understand that I'm better than that and I have to hustle even harder. It made me want to better my Life more and to know that I am a King and I will Walk in my light: Young Simba!

Always Grateful

ife itself is a gift, so always be grateful. It may seem like your life is all bad; you just have to turn that situation into an optimistic one. Both of my parents were great individuals and everything happens for a reason. God makes his soldiers tough with a big heart and a bigger purpose for a reason, and always remember somebody has it worse than you. In high school, I never just thought about college; I was only just trying to get by for the moment. So when we had college fairs come to the school, I wasn't just entertained because I didn't like high school completely, but I knew how to make money. Yes, I came from a broken home so I had to maintain the best way possible. Pressure makes diamonds and it also creates Hustlers. I remember certain holidays where I didn't get much as a child, but they made me appreciate the priceless moments more.{ I remember 1 Christmas where we were going through some things and all I got was some low flat Reebok's and some artificial Jordan 11's that my step-grandfather used to sell called AIR's.

The Jumpman was posting up on the jaunts, lol. It's funny now, but back then, I'm like, Ma what you got going on. Instead of being ungrateful and unappreciative, I laid my outfit out for school the next day and swagged the Reebok jaunts. She already knew I didn't like them, but it made her smile because of my actions.} It made me appreciate the presence of others more and how you should cherish your parents and the free game they are giving you, and it made me want to Help out around the house. I knew in the 8th grade at Geeter middle school I wanted to be an Entrepreneur; my mama knew I shot dice, so instead, she introduced me to selling snacks. She used to take me to this neighborhood store called Macklin's and Granny's market where I used to buy snacks to sell around the school. I had a cooler in the locker, and I used to have this saying "Mane I got chips, juice, drank, and big Texas" what you want? I used to make a killing, one of the teachers approached me one day "Woods you got all that money on you, be careful Mane. Get you a savings". At the time, I wasn't trying to hear none of that until one day I saw a kid get jumped and robbed for everything, including his money and that's when I proceeded to open a bank account. I loved the feeling of having my own money and helping out when I could around the house made me feel great on the inside and like a Boss. I had workers and all, and I made sure they got a piece of the pie as well. I used to make my money then go off to practice, basketball was my gift and tool, but hustling is in my DNA. I come from a family of go-getters, so being my own boss was already instilled in me from day 1.

Betrayal

"They smile in your face, but all the time they want to take your place. Backstabbers."

~ Ojays

Usually, any death in the family reveals true colors. You will outgrow the ones who wounded you and one can't run from Karma. I've been betrayed, and it's usually from the person you think who wouldn't do you like that that does you like that. I had to ask God not to turn me into the people who did me wrong. Being crossed does hurt, but you live and learn as Kings and Queens. I was taught as bad as you want to retaliate sometimes, don't feed into the BS and get tricked out of your spot "ISSA GROWTH". Sometimes you have to Love from a distance because you tend to see the true colors of people, especially the ones that's no use to certain things. Love your enemies and pray for those who persecute you because at the end of this Journey of Life, you can't take any of this shit with you to the grave. If anything, Go to war for your Peace; meditation is probably one of the best things created for the human body. It helps you on all mental levels, it keeps you sane.

Taking time out of your day to sit, relax, and breathe is a Key. Silent your brain and just gather your thoughts. I usually get the best meditation in a quiet place like a car, outside in nature in front of water or usually when I'm in the shower. You are merciful and a child of GOD! We stress about so many things at once, which can cause a mental breakdown. Depression is serious; it can cause you to lose it if you don't have a strong will. Statistically, one out of every sixteen people who are diagnosed with depression, 7 out of 100 males and 1 out of every 100 females will face suicide. The risk is about 20 times that of the general population. Ones with multiple episodes of depression are at greater risk, and people who subside to alcohol or drug addiction are also at high risk. So if you ever felt like this, please understand you are LOVED, get some help, and understand that it's very selfish to put your family in that predicament because they will be the ones hurting the most. One's heart can be so heavy from past/present experiences, so I advise you to just Pray, don't Panic under any circumstance and give it to GOD! There's nothing wrong with going to see a counselor, I did. Not for suicide, thoughts came across but nothing in action ever but after the tragedy of my mom and other dealings, it took everything out of me had me even walking in the dark side; felt like a dark cloud was following me everywhere I went, but that temporary satisfaction that you're getting will not help you, in the long run, it will only hinder you. In the black community, we are prone not to show any feelings that's considered soft or weak, but it's only hurting you in the end.

Have you ever been taken advantage of sexually by a relative and didn't want to speak about it? I have. It's nothing to be ashamed of at all, so speak about it; when I was a kid, I had an older family member who used to babysit me and that's when it happened. I was a child at the time and didn't understand; I could mention the person's name, but I'm not here to bash anybody's character. We had a sit-down discussion with each other, and she was able to admit and say she was sorry. My intentions were to forgive her, but through my actions, I wasn't healed. I was having relations with multiple women looking for satisfaction and masking my real pain. Hurt people hurt people and I'm here to help the next one mentally that may be going through the same shit. Be open to an adult, that childhood trauma that you're constantly balling up and sweeping under the rug hurts you, so speak to someone. My counselor had me doing all types of exercises to help me heal, and I must admit it helped me out a lot. When I go through some shit, I usually take it to the gym with me without trying to get to the root of it. It helps for the moment but once you leave the gym, it resurfaces, take care of your mental health! You can't move forward if you are constantly looking backwards, so Let's Heal!

Faith

When times get hard, you won't be able to see the light, so walk by faith and not by sight.

- Dee Woods.

When you lose your parents, who can you TRUST? So if GOD took your best friend, you feel alone in the world right? They say trust GOD and everything happens for a reason, but once a person is taken, you tend to question GOD like why? But isn't that you not trusting him? We all want to ask WHY sometimes it's life, never lose faith and don't ever give up on Yourself; so you either Quit or Keep going they both hurt G. Tough times don't last, tough people do, and all you need is Faith of a Mustard seed to move a Mountain. Trust is the hardest thing to gain and the easiest thing to lose. I gave trust to people that showed me in the end that didn't deserve it, which we probably all have. Trust is usually earned when actions meet words because One can talk a good game and be living a whole other life. [Trust and Loyalty goes hand to hand; you learn that with your sandbox Negus. You got some real; you got some phony, you got some pythons and then some Jabroni's. Have you ever seen a leech but in human form? Yes, human form; they come in family, friends, associates, and other energy drainers. Your intentions might be genuine but the person that's looking to benefit something from you is a disguised python looking to poison you with a bite multiple times. They will pull you and pull you thinking, "How did I get back in this box" every time you try to run or escape, it pulls you from reaching the top. They will give you every tool to destroy yourself, so keep an attentive eye open. They will try to mislead you by front but don't fall for any of that material shit. It be ALL CAP; I've been in the room with real bosses, the ones you think who wouldn't have it. They either tryna invest, are good at Chess, and know how to dress accordingly. Outside with my peers is where it began, where we got antagonized for skin tone. In today's time, it's usually your mindset that will keep you under and out, not having no motion going but don't be blind by the smoke.]

AmeriKKKa

300+ years of it and we're still living in it even in today's society. Police killing us on tv and walking free with a leave of absence from the job. Quick to draw down on us because we are considered a threat to society. I'm here to tell you not all kids that come from the hood are THUGS! Some of us really want a better life and future and not be stereotyped and categorized. Some of us really want to change the narrative of our story and not be boxed in and judged. Growing up from daycare to middle school, I was mainly around Black people but when I got to Horn Lake High it was diverse even when I got to college. It was kind of a culture shock but It made me adapt and even learn different things from different cultures. Like I said in the beginning I was already taught to treat the janitor just like the CEO so regardless of the race, sex, size I treat you with respect and love. When I got on college campus it was kids from all over, even from out the country and I showed nothing but love and got it in return. The world would be more peaceful if everybody treated everybody with love & respect. I remember an Officer stopped me walking to the gym one morning… "Hey You" I kept walking because I had earphones in, "Hey you" this time I stopped because he pulled his patrol car in front of me. I pulled my earphones out. "What's up" the officer responded "Where you going.." I said to the gym and he pulled off. He later waited until I got closer to my apartment on campus which was by the gym & stopped me again, this time he asked to check my backpack that I was carrying that had nothing but workout equipment in it. I asked what's the problem, he said "You meet the description of a bank robber that was just reported." I looked him in his eyes and I told him, "Why because I'm BLACK? If I was any other race would you have stopped me at all? Probably not. See the first time you pulled in front of me you were expecting me to run as if I committed a crime so you could have a reason. I never gave you a reason and there's nothing suspicious about me walking to the gym at 4 a.m." He gave me my bag back and I told him to have a great day! We live in a world where some officers are supposed to protect and serve but instead are dealing with a lot of fear. You have some that were teased, talked about or even bullied back in high school and now have the opportunity for a lil authority and they try to abuse it. We are all trying to make it back home to our families so stop killing & framing us! I've seen so many stories and read so many books on either an innocent life being taken by an officer that's quick to draw and I've also seen stories of innocent humans that get framed for crimes that they had nothing to do with. You're taking them away from their family… STOP IT that ain't solid. The world will become better, once we TAKE ACCOUNTABILITY. It starts with us first.

Only the Strong Survive

I was born with a chronic lung disease that could cause me to lose my life if not taken seriously. All my life I've been very active in sports and never took it seriously even after being hospitalized for it on multiple occasions. As a child growing up I never wanted to carry my inhaler around because I was concerned of what others would think of me. As I got older I realized my health and being alive is more important than any of that bullshit. I never took asthma seriously until I experienced my first asthma attack. I was gasping for air. I started to take it seriously when my mother passed away from an asthma attack. Asthma is a respiratory disease marked by spasms in the bronchi of the lungs, causing difficulty in breathing. It usually results from an allergic reaction or other forms of hypersensitivity. So this is me telling you if you have asthma please don't take it lightly because it can kill you. Still to this day I'm still able to participate in activities and be able to control it better but it still bothers me from time to time, especially during different climates.

Never let a win get to your head or a loss get to your heart. I've taken so many losses, whether it was a basketball game, money and the biggest of them all Family. Having a strong mind in life is mandatory; one has to be determined to succeed and have it in their mind that nobody or no adversity can stop them. Life is lived daily, but you only die once, but if you live it right once is enough; one can't fail until they quit. One of our biggest problems is that we chase the money and not the dream. I've made mistakes in my past that have matured me into a better person today, and that's life. It's a learning process, but if you are not intelligent enough to learn from your mistakes, then it can ruin the rest of your life. One can't get time back so cherish the moments; a guru once told me "Move with a purpose young one don't be a lost soul out here and patience is a virtue.." and those words stuck with me. See, a wise man will change and a fool will stay the same; the older you get, the wiser you become. Build a strong team but be careful who you let on your ship because some will sink the whole ship because they can't be the captain. You start to find yourself becoming a sponge soaking the game a lot more rather than just talking.

If you are not willing to have self-assessment during growth then you will not make it in the real world, leave your old ways behind, learn from all losses, get comfortable with being alone, and more importantly, Pray for Patience. One has to learn how to never make bad decisions from your emotions; think first! The environment that you are living in doesn't determine who you are but stay HUNGRY! Just because it's raining doesn't mean the Sun isn't going to appear again, and joy definitely wouldn't feel good without pain. See, in life it's 3 P's I live by which is Prayer, Patience, and Perseverance, and when your time finally presents itself, take advantage. With

Covid affecting so many lives and causing a world's large pandemic due to the number of human beings, you must stay hungry towards your purpose or take all your dreams to the graveyard with ya. Evolve or die. If you've ever realized, the only thing on a shark's mind is what: EAT; it stays hungry so one has to be hungry not only towards a Dream but in Life!

Love

There's no love like your parent's love but my grandma Peggy's love was different. Grandma Peggy love was when she cuffs a $20 dollar bill in her hand so only you could see it and grab it. Grandma Peggy love is when you come over to the house on Sunday after church and it's a full soul food plate waiting on you. Grandma Peggy's love was when your friends come over to the house she lets you know "You don't have any friends" and she still welcomes them with open arms and constantly asks them "Are you hungry?" They tell her no they're good and she still makes them a full plate anyway. Grandma Peggy's love was when she goes out her way and gives to a complete stranger. My grandma Peggy taught me the definition of love just by watching, she did it everyday naturally. Before my grandma passed I was more than happy that she was able to see me get my life in order. Before I had my daughter I had two back to back deaths that hit me like a freight train and my grandma Peggy was one of them. Within the same week of my grandma Peggy passing, my daughter Denver was born and my step father was killed. When my daughter was born she was sent to the Newborn intensive care unit. She wasn't adapting at first, her blood sugar was low, so I had to stay a week in the hospital by her side with my fiancée waiting for our daughter to come home. The day she finally came home was the day I had to bury my stepdad so **GOD** knew I needed them both, her Mama and Denver. I was nervous on if I was going to be a great father or not, and before I got engaged I was more than nervous on if I was going to be a great husband or not but my grandma always told me "Just be you baby, you're already covered with love, you've got guardian angels watching you." When my fiancée and daughter came home, my

fiancée was on bed rest so I had to help her a lot around the house, even from basic things like getting out of the bed, putting on clothes, building up her confidence and helping her have patience with herself. Black Women are powerful.

GOD's Love comes first, and then loving yourself. Self-respect, self-esteem, self-confidence, self-value and just being in tune with the star player. Love can be foreign to certain cultures because it's something that many African Americans aren't used to. Are words of affirmation like "I'm Proud of you" "You're doing a great Job" "You're a great mother/father" "Keep up the good work." I feel like once you Respect yourself though the world would be more peaceful, I was always taught to greet the Janitor with the same respect as you greet the CEO. You are not the only person in life that's going through something, be mindful. Life can be very difficult, but one can't fold though. I also feel like a lot of crimes come from hatred because of how that person sees themself. When one life is not going the way that they planned, and a light is being shined through others, it creates jealousy, but you should love Thy neighbors as it's you, clap for others and wait ya turn. We live in a world where we tend to disrespect our women, and it influences the younger group to do the same. You may think the youth are not watching you, but they are, and they are the future. I know sometimes women can go overboard, but would you want somebody to disrespect your Mother, Auntie or sister, stay in your element and think through decisions. Have you ever come across fake love, where a person can tell you "I love you" but actions say otherwise we probably all have. Fake love is arrogant. It doesn't care about what you think and what you feel. They first start off to love you, then they hate you, then they fake love you again it can be contagious so be very Attentive and always LOVE THYSELF!

Keep It Sweven is a brand based on the passion of basketball and other sports while demonstrating life's trials and tribulations to continue to thrive and not let any loss defeat you. It also helps give the youth a positive outlet to continue to be someone. It challenges the young ones mentally as well; through all my personal obstacles on and off the court and also with the negativity of the world, I still managed to graduate college and still am able to be an outlet of some positivity in the world. Yes, I come straight from the hood, a broken home, but you can't let it define you. My life has never been perfect ever, but I wouldn't trade shoes with anybody else because the narrative of this story is authentic, and it's beautiful through the pain and struggle, All Praises to the Most High.

Made in the USA
Monee, IL
10 January 2025

74626964R00030